Manipulation Tactics: Discover How To Exploit the Dark Technique of Manipulation & Learn How To Use It In Your Favor

Aiden Mccoy

© 2015

Disclaimer

Table of Contents

Discover a new power that will take you to the peak of your life, you will have all sorts of situations working under your finger-tips, master the secrets of the best manipulators that ever lived, learn of the daily manipulation tricks used against you, and enjoy as everything unfolds as you intend them.

Introduction to manipulation

Manipulation is the act of intelligently or cleverly convincing or controlling somebody or a group of people to your own favour. The art of manipulation has been there for many centuries it has been used all over history in religion, administration and colonisation of some countries, even know it is used by people, governments, intelligence units, the media and so much more, it is actually as a hidden power by those who are masters in it.

By reading this book, you will be gaining more power and knowledge on how to manipulate without the requirement of special machines or abilities such as palm reading, it is not a daunting or a rigid task as you probably think it is since the chapters have been well revised and laid out for any person regardless age or intelligence quotient (I.Q). A famous writer once said that the power we keep looking for or wishing we had lies in our own hands, we have seen magicians manipulate our minds successfully time after time, for most of us it might have happened in our work areas or relationships together with the media and others, at the end we seemed to be the victims of our own lack of know-how.

There are case studies included that make the book more engaging, they will test your skills in some of the chapters and will sharpen your awareness on the content you learn in some of the chapters in the book.

By completing this book you will also be viewing things in another perspective, an unusual perspective, you will no longer be an item of manipulation, if you wish neither will you be left as you begun the first chapter, it is therefore advisable to be attentive and active in reading without taking holidays, you never know a point might be covered somewhere.

From time begun manipulation has continued being the oldest trick in the book, it has been used in governance, politics, and religion and so much more, here are just a few examples of ways that manipulation has made the world how it is today.

Religion manipulation

An example of a religion whereby manipulation was used is Christianity, Christians believe that in the beginning of humanity, that Eve the woman was manipulated by the serpent to eat the forbidden fruit which she later did.

Photo manipulation

There has been a lot of manipulation in the photo industry since 1987. The invention of the Photoshop occurred in that year, but before that; photo manipulation existed since the 1800s, this was proved by Abraham Lincoln's photo that was altered with a mixture of colours.

Politics manipulation

In the long run politics manipulation is an on-going venture, more like day to day, usually happens when unqualified explanations or rather questionable such as why the price of fuel has shot up despite the world fuel prices going down or why a huge amount of cash has been transferred to an undisclosed account.

As you can see manipulation has its playgrounds and there are so much more in fact if we were to list them down we would come to the conclusion that manipulation exists in every corner. This book wills emphasis on manipulation and how you can activate its power. As we proceed to the steps you will discover more intriguing facts and examples of simple manipulation techniques.

"When you know what a people want, you hold a power against them, you can drive them"

This is an old saying that has stuck its roots to the ground perplexed over the many centuries passed. It describes of one of the abilities of manipulation, and yes no matter what kind of debate there is manipulation is sort of a power since it involves control, manipulation is the key to control.

The world keeps on changing and so do all human behaviours and situations, manipulation has also played a key role, therefore to keep up with the pace the world is moving, it would be wise to be updated on manipulation so as to avoid anybody taking advantage of you, during the fourth coming chapters we shall be focussing more on what, how, when and how it has or can be used effectively, learn of the good and the ugly side of manipulation, learn of how even the mighty are not immune from manipulation, and finally how to manipulate successfully.

Chapter 1: What exactly is manipulation?

Manipulation as viewed in the modern and contemporary World

Manipulation can be defined as cleverly identifying what drives somebody to do what they do and then using that drive as an advantage to either controlling their thoughts or actions. For example lawyers will often look for the key to manipulate a judge and the jury by competing with their opposition on getting the upper convincing hand which is the control key so as the judgeto make a ruling on his favour.

Manipulation can also be referred to as an art or sport since the better an individual is better at it, the better the rewards, the way you can manipulate a dog to bring your newspaper to the house by continuously engaging it in practice by playing fetch won't be the same way you will manipulate a client in business to engage in any business towards your favour, manipulation takes time and skill to be perfect.

Manipulation has no boundaries and by boundaries I mean that it doesn't choose either age or sex, anyone can control you as easily without knowing, this usually proves itself in relationships where there might be a cheating partner or maybe where a certain person brings out the best of mercy and pity emotions in you, this means that the person you either take care of due to pity is either a master in manipulation or might just not be acting up.

Manipulation is a power, anybody can make things or people do as according to what they want, just like puppets take centre stage and are controlled by the puppeteer you can also control circumstances and people, you are the puppeteer in your manipulation playground, and your power can be stronger if you learn how to use and control it. Probably you have noticed that the best manipulators are the best business men and lawyers, for example some years back, a successful business personality namely Donald Triumph manipulated his way to selling the World wrestling Entertainment(WWE) back to its owner for three times as much as he bought it, another example is of an individual who disguised himself as a former veteran and ended up getting luxuriously pampered by the Kenyan government for more than six months, which after was discovered and relieved of the pampering, he successfully got what he wanted via manipulation. "The human race is where everyone is under control by other people, no one controls his own life; the best thing you can ever do is to choose somebody who controls your life with good motive."

Different forms of Manipulation

Psychological manipulation

This mode of manipulation also referred to as emotional manipulation usually involves aggression in form of mental trickery or bullying; this is being justified by the fact that the manipulator is willing to get good results no matter the obstacles. An example of psychological manipulation would be bullying.

Media manipulation

Media manipulation happens when the media; that is the television and radio station, either wants to gain benefits for itself or its clients, for example there might be advertisements made for a specific product, the advertisement is meant to cleverly convince the viewer's so as to purchase the product.

Relationship manipulation

Relationship manipulation is the commonest form there is, it is through many divorces and separations that most people open their eyes and realise that their spouses had been cleverly convincing them, it can also happen between relatives. I have seen relatives take each other to court, for petty reasons that mostly are associated with manipulation. There are simply no boundaries in manipulation.

Crazy making manipulation

In this method the manipulator often instils self-doubt to the victim, crazy manipulation may also cause the victim to believe they are going crazy in one way or another.

Influence shouldn't be regarded as part of manipulation

Influence is the ability of somebody to have an effect on somebody else, for example a good leader will have influence on his followers, his followers will do as he does, if the leader wants his followers to be teachers then he or she will start teaching and without asking or commanding his followers they will follow, the leader can also be said to be the role model.

Manipulation on the other hand is the ability to control people or circumstances to work as to your wishes, it involves playing with circumstances or peoples mind, it therefore shouldn't be confused or taken us manipulation.

Argument on the basis of manipulation

Manipulation can turn out to be good when used with good intent but if otherwise it would be the beginning to a road of deceive, lies and the development of liars, for example we have all witnessed, tried or watched on television manipulation tools such as supernatural human beings with supernatural powers or abilities, they have either impacted our lives with positive or negative influence, we have also seen magicians and most of us can admit to be either once or twice manipulated into their tricks, the truth is, everybody is under a different level of manipulation, the more of a super manipulator you are, the more complex the manipulation you are in, also a famous writer once said that manipulation is like the air we breathe, each day, each second someone is under manipulation, all the abnormal out turn of events is actually the outcome of somebody's result of well-orchestrated manipulation plan, as we go over the book we shall learn of the best manipulation events used in history and how exactly they led to a lot of people believing in them.

Why do people manipulate?

Since the beginning of manipulation in the first century, people have been manipulating and manipulated at different points, manipulation has been done with both good motives and bad motives; here are some of the reasons on why people have either manipulated or why they have decided to be full time manipulators:

a)   To hide their character

If circumstances are to change then it calls for a change in you. That's the motto for most manipulators, to perfectly be a wolf in sheep clothing, the manipulator will act as according to how victims want him to, and this will lead to the manipulator achieving his goals.

b) To blackmail someone

To get to your desired victims servant hood services, you will either have to pay up or look for how you can get the loyalty for free, if you have no money to pay for the servant hood, then just like most manipulators, dig into the life of the victim and get the secret they are cautious about, after getting it, the manipulator confronts the victim and negotiates deals from time to time that he doesn't have to pay for.

c) To introduce to fear

Fear can be taken as an advantage; a manipulator will instil a certain fearful object or natural phenomena that will abstract a victim from reaching or getting across certain boundaries, this in turn will lend the manipulator the upper hand since he will be above the victim.

d) To be cared for

To be taken care of does come with its merits, you can get your chores done and treated in a king like manner, you might even be lucky to get some or all your bills paid for, but after the good treatment and all the pampering comes to an end as a manipulator, you will look for a manipulative way to get the good time back again.

e)   To escape punishment

Punishment is not something that people enjoy doing, besides that it is the best development area that manipulators are bred; we have seen politicians betray each other, corruption allegations being passed from individual to individual, innocent people being prosecuted in courts of law. All and other instances such as this have been manipulation orchestrated.

f)   To escape embarrassment

This is a common reason used in manipulation; the guilty person in this case will do all that he can so that the embarrassment may not befall on him or her, the manipulator might even go to certain extents such as befalling the embarrassment on somebody he wishes.

g)   To get it easily

To get it easily is a statement that I have used to summarize on all the desires that are at the fore front of the manipulator, the manipulator is somebody who is goal oriented and will do anything or rather change any circumstance that comes by his way, for example if the manipulator wants a case charged against him dropped he will plan a manipulation approach which will lead to his desire.

Chapter 2: Myths about manipulation

A myth is a belief held for a long time or a story that tells of a community or people in ancient times surrounded by supernatural beings, they aim at explaining phenomenon or certain beliefs about people.

To explain a manipulation myth, the first step should be to identify the main characteristic of manipulators; that is they are all after something they can't get easily and have to be tricksters to get what they want, in the ancient times the penalties for manipulation would be persecution by hanging, stoning to death or being torched.

Probably you have come across some beliefs like:

1. Manipulation is an evil doing

2. Manipulation happens to only the unwise

3. Manipulation is an act of breaking the law

4. Manipulation is only carried out by lawyers and secret service workers

5. The best time to be manipulated is when you are weak either physically or emotionally

6. Manipulation is just a word to replace lying

7.   Teaching is not a factor in manipulation

8.   A witch is the name given to a manipulation professional

9.   You are above manipulation. Etc...

There are a lot of myths on manipulation but it is good to know that it can turn out to be of great significance if used with good intent and also might turn out to be evil if used for wrong motives. Some of the myths that are described might be true but most of them are false. When it comes to manipulation, we shall be going through some short beliefs and ancient beliefs of manipulation in most genres of the modern world.

When myth says that manipulation is evil, what does it necessarily emphasis?

A lot of people have asked this question time in and time out and still it's debated with the question, is doing evil for the sake of something good result to being viewed as evil? , the word manipulation is not a representation of evil, it also depends on the motive of carrying out the manipulation process, it can't be evil if the outcome is a blessing. For example try and think of killing a sick out of control dog that is prone to bite somebody, would that amount to evil?

Does manipulation only happen to the unwise or ignorant?

Manipulation as explained in the earlier contexts does not choose age or sex, in this case, it also doesn't pick on who is king or citizen, we have even seen big personalities being manipulated, take the example of how the Drug enforcement administration(DEA) works, to catch the cartels in drug trade they usually act as major drug dealers so as to get to them, another example is of a teacher and a student, a student will eventually manipulate a teacher in all sorts of ways especially if there is no work done.

To which degree is manipulation considered an offence?

Manipulation has also being said to be an offence, now an offence can be described as an act of purposely doing wrong, manipulation can either be of good or bad significance, if it is used with intention of resulting to bad, then it is an offence, if it contradicts the law of the land then it can lead to breakage of the law, for example if a party under investigation purposely misleads the judgement of a case. In conclusion, the intentions of the manipulator are what define what kind of a manipulation has been carried out.

Manipulation is only possible by law and business enforcing individuals

If you are amongst the crowd that has accepted that only a certain part of people have the ability to manipulate, then you better scrub the thought out of your mind, anyone can be a manipulator, statistics have even proved that some babies even cry with no reason just for manipulation purposes. Manipulation is something that is learnt in this world mostly naturally and only they that take it as a habit and lifestyle become rulers.

You can choose when to be manipulated and when not to

The statement is just as false as it sounds, in most cases you don't even realise you are being manipulated, whether it's through literature books and songs, the economic position of the country, your faith in religion or other grounds, you never know. The best scenario example where you might not sense any manipulation going on is in relationships with either your boss, fellow workers, workmates, parents, relatives and so much more, as they say, the fighter that won was the one that didn't take any aspect lightly.

Manipulation is just a word to cover up for a string of lies

It might be true in certain circumstances or also be false in other circumstances, for example if a victim was manipulated in a relationship and they claim that manipulation is a string of lies then it they are justified to say so but if a victim found himself or herself parse being tricked for example while entering a contract through manipulation then they have no case and are not deemed to say that there was lying involved.

Teaching is not a factor in manipulation

This is another false statement that has been mythic for a long time now, teaching is not only a factor of manipulation but it's also a manipulation playground, through the many centuries passed, different parts of the world have differently manipulated people to act as according to how the world wants, not only the world but the economy and religion. For the sake of a better future, the young ones are manipulated from today's worldly problems so as to concentrate on how to make the future better. For example centuries ago people would be used as loopholes towards their own nations, through teaching, they would be manipulated to go against their nations, for the better of the other.

Manipulation is a witchcraft thing

Manipulation is not used by witches only; it was during ancient times where civilisation was not easily upheld and most people were ignorant, and for those who were ignorant; carried a belief that manipulation was a supernatural power. Even to some nowadays still belief that only people who proclaim natural abilities such as palm readers are the only ones with the power to manipulate. However, manipulation is a tool that we learn naturally but if we remain ignorant it becomes a myth.

As you can see from the examples above manipulation isn't specifically a myth but more of a misunderstood statement. it emphasises more on the act rather than the actor, decades back in the eighteenth century, the Americans were at war with the Chinese, the Chinese managed to recruit some of the American soldiers, they did this by not forcing them at gun point or torturing them but by manipulating them and turning them against their country. The Chinese can be therefore referred to as the manipulators in that case.

Case study

• James a soldier to his country for ten years, finally caught up with a terrorist that he found hiding in one of the hills that was far from their military base, so far the terrorist had managed to manipulate the guards at the border and successfully got in the field, he seemed to be studying the military from far, so far there was a huge ransom for the terrorist all over the country, James with good motive, shot the terrorist dead. Let's say you are given the opportunity to judge the case, Did James do an evil did? Did it add up to manipulation?

Chapter 3: The manipulator

In this chapter we shall analyse and breakdown the manipulator, get to know how you can be a good manipulator by studying all the strengths that the manipulator has, all the weaknesses they are bound to face, the opportunities that most manipulators still have not discovered, and the threats to the manipulator, after finishing this chapter you should be able to describe the manipulator, and point out every area in his manipulative structure. This will in turn make you a good manipulator and not forgetting it won't be easy for manipulators to manipulate you again.

"and so as to survive they started programming their minds to accept what was to be expected, they stopped thinking before they accepted, they realised that they do not need all that , all they had to do was to find out what others were thinking and also think that too"

Those words speak of nothing but the manipulators, manipulation is just like a sport, the more practise somebody does the better they become, there are different types of manipulators in the world today, varying from workmates, family and even in relationships. Probably you have also once or severally been a manipulator or manipulated in your life knowingly or unknowingly, for example if you have changed outcome of an event for your own benefit by controlling people, know that you are guilty of manipulation, it could have been that magic trick you tried or successfully pulled out and it can also be that gift you got from your spouse, relative or parents that they didn't want to give but you turned the odds, that's also manipulation; but all in all that is passed you shall be opening your mind to new styles that will leave no trace.

By discovering the different types of manipulators we conclude the definition of the manipulator:

The manipulator is the personality that is responsible for manipulating the victim; he is the personality behind the outcome of a certain event, in short he is the person that influences cleverly with the aim of benefiting himself

What makes a good manipulator?

Here are the attributes of the manipulator, it is important to note that good manipulators adapt to new ways everyday just like the mosquito which keeps adapting to different insecticides that are produced from time to time, therefore be vigilant and also take time to discover some of the manipulative ways you have witnessed.

a.   Is confident

In every profession, the best at it are those that are confident in what they do, confidence helps the manipulator by not displaying any gestures or expressions that could jeopardise their goals. If a manipulator acts in a way that brings up questions then chances of achieving his goals will be slim, confidence also helps the manipulator stay calm and successfully execute his desires.

b.   A good actor

Acting is another important aspect that the manipulator should have; the best manipulators are actually the best pretenders and actors, they have that know-how being as their victims wish them to be in terms of their behaviour and thinking.

c.   A good liar

Lying comes hand in hand with manipulation, some people might even confuse. If a manipulator cannot lie confidently then there is no point in trying manipulation, in fact the best manipulators often give samples of truths in lengthy phrases.

d.   Is focused

To achieve success a person must be attentive and visual of his goals; the one that is successful is the one who remained focused no matter what the odds seemed to be. It is therefore essential for a manipulator to be focused on every angle of his work.

e.   Intelligent

The manipulator is said to be clever in his doings, whenever some aspect of his strategy doesn't go to as according to his desires, he will quickly draw up an alternative as a plan B. the manipulator must have first-hand knowledge on his victims, as they say "to manipulate somebody involves the manipulator studying them and discovering what they crave for, in turn the manipulator gives the victim what they crave for then threatens to stop giving"

f.   Will bring out the best or worst in you

Manipulators are able to bring the best in you, if the manipulation is through good motives, they can also bring forth a personality in you that you never knew existed, this is possible since they study their victims well enough and know of what makes them tick, they can either blackmail or lead you to do things you never thought of.

g.   Are masters in creation of illusions

Finally this is one of the most common attributes in manipulation, illusions are false appearances that are meant to effectively help the manipulators succeed, they may be in physical form, and for example the magicians who are deemed the best manipulators use mirrors to manipulate their victim to false belief. Illusions can also be imaginary, for example visions of how the future events will be.

h.   Always has a secret plan

The manipulator works on the basis of a hidden agenda, he is interested in achieving rather than who he betrays to get there, his plan will only be discovered when he meets his goals.

As you can see the manipulator has close characteristics with the liar, but it is important to remember that a liar is based on false statements entirely that are meant to mislead, the manipulator on the other hand is based on cleverly deceiving with the outcome as his benefit. Now we shall look at the daily manipulators and just how they are able to execute their plans daily without leaving a trace.

The daily manipulators

1.   Co-workers

Co-workers are those that you work with, they are the daily people you spend most of your time with. Now how does manipulation work in the working environment?

Basically manipulation as explained in the earlier context is everywhere, each and every one is always under manipulation even those that depend on people working for them are also included. Manipulation in the work area also takes form either as good or bad. However how do co-workers manage to manipulate? And why do they manipulate? Here are some reasons as to why:

a.   For black mail

Blackmail is how somebody gets what they want from another person with the agreement of being discreet on findings of one party, when it comes to co-workers, know that you are dealing with different types of people from different walks of life, there are some individuals that frequently use this tool as a lifestyle, a co-worker can blackmail by ordering his workmate to do all the work, he can also blackmail for some other reason. it is therefore an advantage to the manipulator and disadvantage to the manipulated.

b.   To eliminate your chances of getting a promotion

Promotions are what every worker dreams of; no worker wants to remain in the same position earning the same figure for the rest of their entire life, to get a promotion co-workers will plan against each other they will manipulate each other but the overall manipulator will be the winner. To get a promotion in a competitive environment calls for good skills in manipulation.

c.   To get you dismissed

That's right! Don't think you are too safe in the working area, know that people are not the same and some will want you out, they will either manipulate you to mistakes or manipulate the boss to see some negativity in you.

d.   To have control over you

Manipulation as discussed earlier is based on the fact that somebody who is the manipulator wants to be in charge of you, to be in charge will result to the authoritative person gaining control over you. The manipulator will therefore have more time to relax as he or she controls you to perform their work.

e.   To transfer their duties or punishments to you

Manipulation will lead to people suffering for others, the manipulator when in trouble and realises that all odds are against him, he or she will quickly find a target and plan in such a way to transfer his punishments to somebody else.

The examples above on how co-workers manipulate each other are not exhausted, you can also brain storm and come up with other ways, as explained earlier it is important to keep up with the pace that manipulators are inventing.

Ways to avoid being manipulated by the manipulative co-workers

- **Being vigilant and attentive**

Study the normal behaviours of your co-workers so that you will know when they are acting strange. This will help you to identify instances where there is manipulation.

- **Stay professional**

If you do your work professionally, the manipulators will find it difficult to manipulate you since you will have no loopholes that they could exploit.

- **Learn to say 'NO'**

Most manipulators in the workplace approach those that easily accept anything they are requested to do, now saying no shouldn't be to all requests but you should have an open mind and take time to thinkabout it so as to accept or decline.

- **Be clear and walk your talk**

Make sure that you do as you proclaim, be a person of integrity and by showing of these actions, you will scare the manipulative co-worker away.

2. The boss as the manipulator

A manipulative boss is one that is dangerous, he is also referred to as the Machiavellian boss, as common with all manipulators is that he has a secret plan and is focused more, he will not be comfortable to work with. Working with the manipulative boss means that you are being used to meet his goals, nothing more.

How will the boss manipulate you?

a. By asking simple questions

The boss will tend to ask small simple questions about you so that he may have an upper handto you use against you in the future.

b.   He will take credit for your hard work

The boss will endlessly praise himself with regards to work you have done. He will make up theories on how he did not require your help to be where he is.

c.   Blame you for his or her mistakes

Working with a manipulative boss means that you are just a tool, he will therefore use you as the tool to blame his mistakes in a manipulative manner.

d.   Deception

Most bosses that have been associated with corruption and not paying employees fall into the manipulative bosses' category. They will tell you what you need to hear all in the name of achieving their goals, they will manipulate you as much as possible by deceive to reach their targets.

e.   Shaming

This happens when the boss either publicly or via notice confronts you, as the boss shames you he is actually getting the sense of feeling of superiority and king of the jungle. This can be de-motivating and humiliating if done publicly, the boss might even be doing this for the main purpose of manipulating you to leave.

How to deal with manipulative bosses

- **Be clear and specific on your relationship**

Let your boss realise and if not draw a clear line to where your relationships stops. Do not let the manipulative boss be too close, remember he has a secret plan and is looking for information to use against you.

- **Be aware of your rights**

Every human is entitled to rights, there is a certain level where people should not cross, and to give an example is a threat that is sufficient to be a tort. The bottom line is, if you let your boss walk over you then you will be allowing him or her to manipulate you.

- **Be brave**

Manipulative bosses have a bully like quality in them, if you show a bully that you are afraid of them, they will use your fear as an advantage, the manipulative boss is likewise, do not accept haphazardly anything he requests with an excuse of safeguarding your job. Remember he or she is a manipulator.

- **Be a professional**

Do your work and make sure that all you do is as stipulated in your contract, if you do your job correctly and as according to contract, your boss will not be able to manipulate you.

3. A family member as amanipulative person

The family member can manipulate you by either using your own guilt, fear or kindness against you, everybody in the family from the parents to the infants has ability to influence, I remember way back when one of my friends who was taking care of their dying mother wrote to me, she was not happy with the thought that she was manipulated. Apparently she had been forced to leave work early by a phone call she received that her dying grand mother had refused to eat. The grandmother claimed that she just needed to see her granddaughter who had not visited her for long. She took advantage of her physical well being to manipulate her daughter to visit her. In turn the daughter was angry. She felt the common feeling that the manipulated feel,anger.

How to deal with manipulative family members

- **Let not your kindness be your weakness**

Learn how to set boundaries when it comes to kindness, you might be too kind and polite which are the main characteristics manipulative people find in their victims.

- **Learn to say NO**

Manipulative people are demanding people; they will keep demanding more from you, if you will not be able to stand up for yourself and say no, then you will end up being manipulated which is not a good thing.

- **Be aware and know all about manipulators**

As they say, iron sharpens iron; the best way to catch a thief is to pretend you are a thief, the same applies to manipulators, and you can easily identify manipulation by studying about manipulators.

3. Manipulators in relationships

Especially in spouse to spouse relationships manipulation is a common factor, one spouse can be the manipulator or better yet both can do the manipulation. Be it any type of relationship, anybody is vulnerable relationships can be based on relatives, children or even friends, anybody is vulnerable. In this case we shall be viewing spouse to spouse manipulation.

Exactly how are spouses manipulated?

a. Cheating

Cheating is whereby a spouse in relationships has another spouse outside the relationship; the spouse cheating in this case is the manipulator.

b. Lying

Lying is an act that goes hand in hand with manipulation, it involves one of the spouse intentionally misleading by giving false information.

c.   Deceive

Deceive is betrayal, the manipulator in this case is the one that does the opposite of an agreement the couple made together.

How to deal with manipulators in relationships

•   End the relationship

A manipulator is not someone who started cleverly convincing people seconds ago, manipulation is just like a sport and takes time to perfect, if a partner is found guilty of manipulation, know its hard for the person to completely get over it and might end up doing it again.

•   Don't blame yourself

The worst thing you can ever do is blame yourself for somebody's acts, focus on yourself and don't blame yourself, blaming yourself will be part of being manipulated.

- **Be aware and well acknowledged on the behaviours of the manipulator**

Ignorance is costly, and by costly I do not mean that it is in monetary terms, it is costly in such aspects as pain. The more you know about the manipulators lifestyle and behaviours, the more you save yourself from the aftermath of manipulation. You will also be able to detect any early signs of manipulation and gain the upper hand.

Chapter 4: The manipulated

The manipulated are the victims of the manipulator; they are the ones that have been cleverly convinced to do something or to help out in achieving the manipulator's goals.

How the manipulator succeeds in manipulating is brought about by some factors that are also referred to as the characteristics of the manipulator's prey or in this case the victims. Such factors include:

- **Low self confidence**

Most of the victims have proved to be of low self-confidence, one of the adaptations of the manipulators is that they exhibit a high sense when it comes to confidence; the manipulator is somehow a bully.

- **Strong urge to be popular**

Popularity is when everybody knows you; it's more of being a celebrity, most victims will be manipulated using this trick, especially the teenagers. If a person wants to be popular, the manipulator will use the "want to be popular" excuse as a tool to control the victim.

- **Loneliness phobia**

The victims of the manipulator are lonely people, they will accept being manipulated as long as the manipulator doesn't leave them, this might be linked to suffering from low self-esteem.

- **Ignorant**

Victims usually discover they were ignorant after the manipulator has finished deceiving and they are now paying for it; they are ignorant of the signs of manipulation and also ignorant that there can be an outcome of deception.

- **Say yes to everything**

The manipulated have the habit of accepting anything, they are unable to stand for their selves and say no to the manipulator, an example is of those who accept working beyond hours without being paid overtime, these are the favourites of the manipulative bosses.

- **Are over polite and over-kind**

Over polite meaning that they will accept being walked on without arguing and over kind meaning they will help even if they are too tired to do it, these kinds are the ones that turn out to be the parents that spoil their children.

Test yourself if you are among the manipulated by answering the following:

1.   **Do you lack self-confidence?**

Self-confidence means if you have faith in yourself, if you believe in yourself.

2.   Are you unable to say no?

Has your boss asked you to start a new project on a Friday night and you accepted, remember it was after working hours, or rather has any of your relations asked you to do something you didn't like and you did it?

3.   Are you constantly in search of approval or acceptance?

In search of acceptance meaning that you will do anything to get the attention of either your peers or those within your relations, approval meaning that in everything you do, you except feedback from your peers.

4.   Is somebody blackmailing you?

It could be a workmate or one of your close relations, are you living in fear that they withhold information which would turn around your life, if so then that is another characteristic you have in being the manipulated.

5.   Do you often feel guilty of somebody else's mistakes?

Most manipulated victims tend to be heavy hearted when it comes to matters as to regards the welfare of the manipulator, they might even exhibit secure characteristics to hide the manipulators tracks.

6.   Do you suspect infidelity in your relationship?

If your relationship spouse portrays suggestive behaviour or has changed suddenly, you might find yourself as a victim of manipulation.

Chapter 5: The manipulation process and techniques

The manipulation process is how a victim is cleverly convinced to indulge in an activity whose outcome will benefit the manipulator but leave the victim manipulated. As pointed out in the earlier chapters there are many qualities of both the manipulator and manipulated.

However, the manipulation process involves technique, an unplanned approach to manipulation will lead to failure, here we will be learning about the different styles that the manipulator uses to successfully execute his hidden plan, these techniques are:

1.   **Acting as the victim**

This process involves the manipulator pretending to be victim of an offence, by acting as the victims they gain pity and sympathy from their victims.

2. Promising their victims gain

The manipulators are able to colourise their victim's dreams and promising them they either help them get to their desires or get their desires to them, they decorate the end for the victim to be so attractive and gaining.

3. Scaring

Scaring can take the form of blackmail or bullying, the manipulators forcefully demand for services from their victims, but in blackmail the victims are usually willing to hand over their services with the agreement that the manipulator will be silent.

4. Promising that the victims will not loose

The manipulator in this case will have studied his victim and known what they fear losing, he in turn uses this as a tool by promising the victim that they have nothing to lose through the process.

5.   Seducing

This is when the manipulator takes the guard off the victim by praising or rewarding them, after their take out their guard the manipulator then does what he is best at i.e. cleverly convincing.

6.   Lying

As explained in most of the earlier context, lying goes hand in hand with manipulation, the manipulator is a master of lies and when he lies he leaves no trace, the truth comes to life when it cannot change any circumstance.

7.   Confusing

Manipulation is an art that in involves cleverly misleading.by confusing the victim the manipulator will strike his plan.

8.   Pretending

The manipulator mostly pretends that they no anything, this is part of the manipulators strategy as the victim will tell everything and try to explain of their plan, in turn the manipulator will use the information to his advantage.

Chapter 6: How to use manipulation in your favour

Manipulation is power, with power you can achieve more than you ever thought, by having power of control to people, results and events will turn out towards your favour.

There are a lot of ways to use manipulation, but it is encouraged to be ethical and use them only for good motives. Here are some of the ways to use manipulation towards your favour:

a.   If you can't convince them confuse them

Mastering manipulation will not only help you in improving your skill in convincing but also help you win debates, you will be able to quickly analyse the odds and come up with a perfect confusion plan.

b.   Save yourself from going through events that are not towards your favour

For example if you analyse future events and they are not reflecting your interest, manipulation can help you not go through this events since you can evade by changing the circumstances.

c.   You can be a role model

People will admire how everything just works into your favour, they will want to associate with you as they see that you always achieve.

d. You will gain the upper hand in every position you are placed

Manipulators are often leaders, they have the ability to change circumstances to their favour, and it is through manipulation that you will find yourself getting promotions from time to time.

e. Manipulation makes you a valuable asset

It is through manipulation that you hold information on everyone, you know what makes them and how they will react, and they are your puppets and will always depend on you.

f. Manipulation makes you charming

You can easily transform to what your victims except of you, you will know what to say and what to do to convince and change your image to what the victim desires.

g.   Your work will be done for you

You can manipulate your way to a fun- work- free life; it is through manipulation that you will know how to work smart; you will also be able to cleverly convince your workmates to do your work.

h.   **Discover your self-worth**

Manipulation will help improve your esteem, you will be able to manage your emotions and balance them to portray a strong wise personality.

When manipulation doesn't work

If for some reason manipulation doesn't work and probably you have been discovered as a manipulator, remain calm and don't defend yourself, let the accusers condemn you, do not even try to use any manipulation techniques, after interrogation is over you can then point out some aspects that will bring out doubt to the accusers, these will lead to raise of questions and they will start losing confidence in their findings.

Manipulation will not work under the following conditions:

a.   The manipulator fails to plan accordingly

b.   The victim discovers that they are being manipulated

c.   The manipulator chooses a victim that does not have the qualities of the manipulated

d.   The manipulator fails to follow his script

Conclusion

Manipulation is an art that has its professionals and legendaries; it takes a lot of time and practice to master the fine art, manipulation doesn't require any special abilities or equipment, it is a natural effect, it begins at a young age and if followed through grows into a masterpiece, there are also different types of manipulation ranging from relationships to psychological to so much more, therefore being vigilant is essential, in fact everyone is under manipulation, even the manipulators themselves can also be manipulated by any person regardless of family or relative.

Manipulation has both its prows and cones, not all manipulation is bad or as some people says evil, manipulation can either be good or bad depending on the motive at hand, therefore if its good then that means the motive was of significance but if it turned out to be bad then it was executed with bad motives.

For the well-being of good relationships and the world, it is important that people refuse to be ignorant of manipulation whether good or bad, being ignorant not only is it considered as bliss but can also be expensive in the long run.

Manipulation is a power tool that will transform mentally, manipulators have high esteem, they are leaders, and they have the ability to change ma circumstance quickly. However, they are good in lying and will take advantage of anyone to get to their goals.

By mastering the manipulation techniques and the qualities of ma good manipulator, many opportunities will come knocking at the door, you will no longer have to look for them.

www.ingramcontent.com/pod-product-compliance
Lightning Source LLC
Chambersburg PA
CBHW070818290526
45795CB00002B/747